WEST END BRANCH
MAY   2001

8x 5/18 - W
8x10/24 W

J
979.473 MARGARET
Margaret, Amy
Mission Santa Clara de
Asis /

S0-AWV-869

WITHDRAWN

The Missions of California

Mission
Santa Clara de Asís

Amy Margaret

ALAMEDA FREE LIBRARY
2200-A Central Avenue
Alameda, CA 94501

The Rosen Publishing Group's
PowerKids Press™
New York

To Danielle and Andrew, teachers I love and admire.

Published in 2000 by The Rosen Publishing Group, Inc.
29 East 21st Street, New York, NY 10010

Copyright © 2000 by The Rosen Publishing Group, Inc.
All rights reserved. No part of this book may be reproduced in any form without permission in writing from the publisher, except by a reviewer.

Photo Credits and Photo Illustrations: pp.1, 4, 26, 33, 35, 36, 37, 42, 48, 49a, 49b, 49c, 50, 51 by Cristina Taccone; pp. 6a, 11, 19, 44 © The Granger Collection; pp. 6b, 21, 22a, 22b, 32 © Superstock; p. 7 Courtesy of National Park Service, Cabrillo National Monument; p.10 © Digital Stock; p. 12 by Michael K. Ward; pp.15, 47 CORBIS/Bettmann; pp. 16, 25, 31 Santa Barbara Mission Archive - Library; p. 18 © The Bridgeman Art Library; p. 27 Department of Special Collections, University of Southern California Libraries; p. 40 Seaver Center for Western History Research, Los Angeles County Museum of Natural History; p. 43 by Tim Hall; pp. 52, 57 by Christine Innamorato.

First Edition

Book Design: Danielle Primiceri

Layout: Michael de Guzman

Editorial Consultant Coordinator: Karen Fontanetta, M.A., Curator, Mission San Miguel Arcángel
Editorial Consultant: Russell K. Skowronek, Ph.D., Associate Professor of Anthropology
            Department of Anthropology and Sociology, Santa Clara University,
            Santa Clara, CA 95053
Historical Photo Consultants: Thomas L. Davis, M. Div., M.A.
            Michael K. Ward, M.A.

Margaret, Amy
    Santa Clara de Asís / by Amy Margaret. — 1st ed.
        p. cm. — (The missions of California)
    Includes bibliographical references and index.
    Summary: Traces the history of this California mission with reference to the Spanish explorers, Franciscan and Jesuit missionaries, Ohlone Indians, and its secularization by the state.
    ISBN 0-8239-5494-3 (lib. bdg.)
    1. Santa Clara Mission—History—Juvenile literature. [1. Santa Clara Mission—History. 2. Missions—. California.] I. Title. II. Series.
    F869.S47M37 1999
    979.4'73—dc21   99-17433
                                                              CIP

Manufactured in the United States of America

Contents

Exploring California

Today the state of California is home to a wide variety of cultures, including people of Asian, Filipino, Irish, African-American, and Scandinavian descent. It was not always so heavily populated with people from many different backgrounds and ethnicities. Before the Gold Rush in 1849, California had few visitors. Its primary inhabitants were California Indians, who lived in hundreds of different tribes up and down the coast. The California Indians were hunters and gatherers and survived by living off the land for thousands of years. Their lives were changed dramatically by the arrival of Spanish colonists, who built a chain of 21 missions along the California coast. These missions now house some of the best preserved artifacts of California Indian craftmanship.

Mission Santa Clara de Asís was the eighth mission founded by the Spanish and one of the first Spanish missions in the northern region of California. Each mission was started in hopes of attracting local California Indians to live and work at the mission and to convert to Christianity. The land around Mission Santa Clara de Asís was home to tribes of Ohlone Indians.

Spanish Catholic missionaries, who hoped to spread their religion to the California Indians along the coast, founded the missions of California. A mission is a place where people go to teach others about a certain religion and other aspects of a foreign way of life or culture. The first California mission was built in 1769. By 1823, there were 21 missions along the coast of California, stretching from San Diego to San Francisco.

◀ *Mission Santa Clara de Asís attracts thousands of tourists each year.*

The Exploration Age

The 1400s and 1500s were a time of European exploration of places all over the world. European governments were eager to find riches and search for more land.

Spain was one of the first countries in Europe to make exploration a priority. Spain sent Christopher Columbus to try and circumnavigate, or circle, the globe.

Columbus explored the Americas.

In 1540, Francisco Vásquez de Coronado was the first to explore what is today the southwestern United States. Some Spanish explorers, such as Hernán Cortés, did more than just look for gold and other riches. From 1519 to 1521, Cortés led Spanish soldiers to conquer the Aztecs, who had occupied the land for thousands of years in what is today called Mexico. The Spanish named this land New Spain. Juan Rodríguez Cabrillo and Sebastián Vizcaíno

were the first two Spanish explorers to sail north from New Spain, up the coasts of Baja (lower) California and Alta (upper) California. From these travels, Spain hoped to expand its empire around the globe.

Cortés conquered the great Aztec empire in the land that is today Mexico.

Juan Rodríguez Cabrillo

Juan Rodríguez Cabrillo, who served with Cortés, was the first Spanish explorer sent from Spain to explore the western coast of North America. His primary goal was to find a river that joined the Pacific and Atlantic Oceans. He and his crew were also supposed to look for harbors where Spanish ships could rest on their long trips. In 1542, Cabrillo and his crew sailed from New Spain, up the western coast into Alta California. (Today, Alta California is the state of California and Baja California is part of Mexico.) When Cabrillo sighted Alta California, he claimed these coastal lands for Spain.

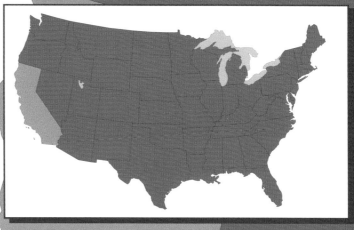

◄ *Cabrillo traveled up the coast of Alta California.*

○ San Francisco de Solano
○ San Rafael Arcángel
○ San Francisco de Asís
○ San José
○ Santa Clara de Asís
○ Santa Cruz
○ San Juan Bautista
○ San Carlos Borromeo del Río Carmelo
○ Nuestra Señora de la Soledad
○ San Antonio de Padua
○ San Miguel Arcángel
○ San Luis Obispo de Tolosa
○ La Purísima Concepción
○ Santa Inés
○ Santa Bárbara
○ San Buenaventura
○ San Fernando Rey de España
○ San Gabriel Arcángel
○ San Juan Capistrano
○ San Luis Rey de Francia
○ San Diego de Alcalá

The ships sailed as far north as the area that is today the state of Oregon. Their journey helped prove that Alta California was not an island as the Spanish had thought, but a large mainland. Cabrillo died on the voyage. He is considered by many to be the first European explorer of the California coast.

Nobody knows for sure how the state of **California** got its name. Some historians believe that when early Spanish explorers first saw the California land, they thought it was an island, so they named it after a fictional queen, Califia, who ruled an island. Another theory is that the name California comes from *califaco*, which is the Latin word for warm.

Sebastián Vizcaíno

In 1602, Spanish explorer Sebastián Vizcaíno was sent by ship to continue Cabrillo's search for a connecting waterway between the Atlantic and Pacific Oceans. This trip was Vizcaíno's first attempt to land along Baja California's rocky shore. Cabrillo had been the only explorer to successfully make it to land.

An experienced sailor, Vizcaíno and his ships sailed northward and came upon a safe harbor, which Vizcaíno named Monterey, after the viceroy of New Spain. Based on Vizcaíno's records, it was around this area that the Ohlone tribespeople first saw the Europeans. With signs and hand gestures, the Ohlone Indians were friendly to the visitors, giving them food that they had gathered and entertaining them with dances. Less than 200 years later, the descendants of these Ohlone Indians would build Mission Santa Clara de Asís and provide Spanish soldiers, missionaries, and themselves with food through a thriving agricultural system.

Vizcaíno returned to New Spain, unsuccessful in his primary goal of finding a water route connecting the Atlantic and Pacific Oceans. The viceroy did not think the time or money invested made future trips worthwhile, so Spain decided to stop funding these voyages overseas. No Spanish ships sailed to California for the next 160 years.

In the meantime, both Russia and England started sending ships to the Pacific coast of North America. Spain became concerned that it would lose the land that Cabrillo and Vizcaíno had claimed. Spanish rulers took measures to permanently control the Alta California land and to rule over the American Indians who occupied it.

The Ohlone Indians

Long before Cabrillo or Vizcaíno sailed their ships along the California coast or Catholic friars began plans to build missions, many different California Indian tribes were already in the area. The tribal group closest to the Santa Clara area were the Ohlone.

There were many Ohlone tribes, spreading from the San Francisco area to south of Monterey Bay. It was not unusual for members of tribes living within a few miles of each other to speak different languages. They had no written form of communication.

The Ohlone men hunted for food, searching for deer, antelope, ducks, and geese. The Ohlone also fed on the abundance of seafood from the ocean, as well as berries, mushrooms, grass seeds, and other plants they found growing in the area.

One of the Ohlone's most important food staples was acorns. There were different types of acorns growing in the northern region of Alta California, and the Indians took advantage of them all. The Ohlone ground the acorns into flour, which was then used to make porridge, biscuits, and soup.

◀ *The Ohlone hunted deer for food.*

Ohlone Indians often decorated themselves with paint for ceremonies. ▶

10

Village Life

Every village had an assembly house and a *temescal*, or sweathouse. The assembly house was made of tule, which were tightly woven reeds used to block out rain and wind. This building was used for large gatherings and could hold the entire village population. The *temescal* was a small hut used by members of the tribe to cleanse their bodies through sweating. *Temescals* are similar to today's saunas. The Ohlone went through this ritual for a variety of reasons, such as healing an illness, curing a skin disease, or preparing for a hunt or a religious ceremony. Individual homes for the tribespeople were constructed from wooden posts and were covered with tule.

Every village had a shaman and a chief. The shaman was the religious leader who healed sick people. The chief, who could be either male or female, was one of the wealthiest in the village. His or her wealth, passed down from generation to generation, was used for the benefit of the entire village and those in need. Whenever a visitor came to the village, it was the responsibility of the chief to feed him well and give him gifts. The chief also led hunts for food.

The elderly people in the Ohlone tribe were treated with great respect. When they had something to say, the younger people listened carefully. The chief made sure all the needs of the elderly, such as food and shelter, were taken care of.

Children were cherished and were raised not just by the mother and father, but by the extended family, including aunts, uncles, and grandparents. Children had lots of time to play and enjoy their natural surroundings. They were not expected to work until they reached puberty.

Ohlone Skills

Ohlone men were skilled hunters. Their most prized possessions were the bows they crafted by hand. A hunter could take 10 days to perfect his bow. Arrowheads made from rocks and a natural glass called obsidian, were shaped by hand. All weapons and tools were made from wood, stones, shells, or animal bones.

Ohlone women were equally gifted in basket weaving. The Ohlone women made baskets that were beautiful enough to display in any museum. In fact, some are exhibited in different museums and libraries around the world today. These handwoven baskets were a necessity for the Ohlone women, as baskets were used for almost every daily chore. Women used the baskets to shake and separate seeds from plants, to carry and store water, to cook food, and to carry almost any load.

The Ohlone were calm and easygoing people. They lived by three rules: work hard, do not complain, and behave in a good way. They lived freely and peacefully. Their daily lives did not require a lot of structure. Their quiet way of life may have made it easier for the missionaries to step into the Ohlone villages and encourage the Indians to join mission life.

When the Spanish government decided to move into the territory where the California Indians lived, it planned to develop a mission system. Spain had already developed a mission system to build up New Spain, particularly the Baja California area.

The Spanish Mission System

In the mid-1700s, Spanish rulers were eager for the Catholic friars to build missions. The missions were part of larger settlements, which were made up of three branches: religious, military, and civic. The Catholic missions, the religious branch, were to be built first to attract the local Indians. Some Indians joined the missions voluntarily. However, many Indians were forced to leave their villages against their will and live on the mission sites. The Indians who came to the mission were taught trades to help keep the mission running smoothly. The missionaries taught the Indians about Christianity and then baptized them. Baptism is a ritual, performed with water, that is held when someone is accepted into the Christian faith. Once the California Indians were baptized into the Catholic faith, they were called neophytes.

The Spanish government planned to build a mission in the south (San Diego), then in the north (Monterey) of Alta California. Missions would be built between these missions and as far north as Sonoma. As they were built, they formed El Camino Real, a road that stretches 700 miles along California's coast. Its name means "The Royal Road" or "The King's Highway," after King Carlos III of Spain.

The Spanish would then build presidios, sometimes with the help of local Indians. Presidios were military forts for the soldiers. Each presidio's function was to house soldiers who would protect the Spanish settlers of the mission, watch over the Indians at the mission, and enforce Spanish laws. The Spanish would also develop *pueblos*, or agricultural towns, outside the missions.

This picture shows neophytes being baptized. ▶

It was thought that Mission Santa Clara de Asís would be given to the neophytes after 10 years.

The goal was for the California Indians to eventually be able to run these settlements on their own. Spanish missionaries figured it would take 10 years to establish each settlement. Spanish rulers assumed the California Indians would become loyal Spanish citizens, thus expanding the Spanish empire even further. At that time, the Spanish soldiers and missionaries would move on to establish more missions in other areas, and the Indians would be left to live on their own. This process is called secularization, which means that the church would turn over the mission land to citizens who were ruled by the government rather then by the church. Although the missions did end up being secularized, it did not happen the way the Spanish had originally planned.

To expand their empire and build a new land, the Spanish needed more than a well-developed plan. They needed California Indians, like the Ohlone. With only two missionaries and five or six soldiers per mission, the Indians' labor was necessary in order to build the missions and keep them running.

The Founders of Mission Santa Clara de Asís

In addition to the thousands of Ohlone Indians who played a role in making Mission Santa Clara de Asís one of the most successful California missions, there were a few key figures who were critical to the founding of the Santa Clara mission.

Fray Junípero Serra

Fray Junípero Serra, known as the founder of the California mission system, was born Miguel José Serra in 1713. He spent his childhood on Majorca, an island off the coast of Spain. His parents made education

a priority for Miguel José and sent him to a school taught by Franciscans. Franciscans are an order of Catholic friars. They are called Franciscans because they live by the Christian example set by Saint Francis of Assisi. Franciscans wear brown woolen robes tied at the waist with a piece of white rope. Their feet are bare except for sandals. When a person joins the Franciscan brotherhood, he promises, or takes a vow, never to marry, never to seek material wealth, and always to act in total obedience to the Christian god. While studying with these learned religious men, Miguel José

▲
Saint Francis of Assisi was the founder of the Franciscan Order.

18

▶ *Fray Serra founded 9 of the 21 Alta California missions.*

F. Junípero Serra

also decided that he wanted to become a missionary. A missionary travels to foreign lands telling people about Christianity in an effort to convert them.

Miguel José went on to graduate from the Convent of San Francisco, becoming a Franciscan friar, or *fray* in Spanish. He was now entitled to pick a new name for himself. He named himself Junípero, after a man who had been very close to Saint Francis. For the next six years, he continued his studies to become a priest at another convent in Palma, called Saint Francis.

Once he became a priest, Fray Junípero Serra remained at Saint Francis. He taught classes and ran the convent's library. In 1749, he and two of his former students, Fray Francisco Palóu and Fray Juan Crespí, had the chance to follow their dreams of missionary work. Catholic friars were needed in New Spain. Even though the site was thousands of miles from home and they would probably never see Majorca again, they enthusiastically boarded the ship for the long journey. Sailing across the Atlantic Ocean to New Spain, the three missionaries knew this was a rare opportunity that they could not pass up. They had heard of the American Indians who lived in the place that the Europeans called the New World (North, Central, and South America). Serra couldn't wait to share his religion with the Indians, people who had never heard about Christianity. Many people in Europe believed the Indians were "uncivilized" because they did not live their lives in a way that the Europeans believed was appropriate. Today, we know this is far from the truth. The California Indians had their own interesting and successful culture, one that kept them happy and healthy for generations. We have also learned to appreciate the value of diversity, embracing, rather than judging, other cultures.

Once Serra, Palóu, and Crespí arrived in the port city of Veracruz, New Spain, they still had close to 260 miles to go before reaching Mexico City.

▲

Fray Serra first went to Veracruz before traveling to Mexico City.

Biographers estimate that Serra traveled more than 24,000 miles through California to establish and maintain the missions. That is more than Marco Polo's journey and the trek of Lewis and Clark combined!

New Spain

The three missionaries spent about 14 days traveling to reach the College of San Fernando in Mexico City. (It would take about eight hours of driving in a car to cover the same distance.)

The weather was extremely hot, and the wool robes the friars wore made it feel even hotter. The sand from the trails probably got into their open-toed sandals as they walked, creating even more discomfort. Yet, the friars never complained. They were familiar with hardship and accepted it as part of their life's work.

One evening, an insect bit Fray Serra on his foot. The bite quickly infected Serra's foot and spread pain throughout his leg. Serra's pain soon became unbearable and the missionaries stopped their long trek for one day. The following day, Serra convinced his travelmates that, despite his pain, he was well enough to continue. Serra endured pain in his leg that caused him to limp for the rest of his life. As he grew older and continued his travels throughout Alta California, his limp grew worse.

Once Serra arrived in Mexico City in January 1750, he spent the next 17 years fulfilling various duties at the College of San Fernando.

Baja California and Alta California

In 1767, Fray Serra was chosen to supervise the 15 existing Spanish missions in Baja California, which is today northwestern Mexico. Serra worked hard to keep the Franciscan missionaries who ran each individual mission happy. He tried to visit each mission at least once each year to make sure the friars had everything they needed. A year later, Spain claimed Alta California for its own. This event changed Fray Serra's life.

When talks began of planning new missions in the uncharted Alta California, Serra was the best candidate to head up this large undertaking. Finally, Serra's dream would come true. He would have the opportunity to travel to places never visited by other missionaries.

Serra was involved in the founding of the first nine California missions, though explorers such as Gaspár de Portolá and Captain Don Juan Bautista de Anza helped him choose the actual sites.

23

Gaspár de Portolá

In 1769, the viceroy of New Spain appointed Gaspár de Portolá to lead a group to establish settlements in Alta California. Portolá sent two ships and two walking expeditions to San Diego. Fray Serra accompanied Portolá on one of the land groups, which left in March 1769. On July 16, 1769, Fray Serra founded California's first mission, Mission San Diego de Alcalá. This was to be the first permanent European settlement in California.

As Serra and his companions planned new mission sites, they looked for areas with plenty of fresh water, fertile soil for planting crops and feeding livestock, and a supply of wood for building structures and furniture.

Most important for the missionaries and for the Spanish rulers, the area needed to be inhabited by large groups of California Indians. The missionaries wanted to be near tribes in order to teach them about Christianity. They also needed the Indians to help them build the mission and do all the chores to maintain the mission's productivity and success.

Don Juan Bautista de Anza

In 1774, Spain sent the explorer Captain Don Juan Bautista de Anza to further investigate the California coast. After his initial trek along the coast with a small group of men in January 1774, Anza hurried back to Mexico City to plan a larger trip. He wanted to reach the northern San Francisco Bay and bring a large group of people along to settle the area.

In October 1775, Anza set off with about 240 people, including settlers, soldiers, and Franciscan friars. In March, he reached Monterey, where many people stayed to build homes. Anza, along with a Catholic friar, continued northward to select sites for a presidio. They chose mission sites around the San Francisco Bay area, including the land where Mission Santa Clara de Asís would be built about two years later.

Mission Santa Clara de Asís was built near San Francisco Bay. This is a drawing of the mission around 1830.

The Founding and Building of Mission Santa Clara de Asís

The Beginning of Mission Santa Clara de Asís

Two years after Don Juan Bautista de Anza located the site for Mission Santa Clara de Asís, a founding ceremony was held by Fray José Murguía and Fray Tomás de la Peña. For the first service that cold wintry day in January 1777, Peña constructed a small, sheltered altar and held Mass. A wooden cross was also built and hammered into the soil to mark the site.

The friars prepared a report, called an *informé*, of everything they had received from New Spain and the other nearby missions to help the Santa Clara mission get started. The list included: 2 plowshares, 4 crowbars, 36 hoes, 12 digging sticks, 24 axes, 12 machetes, 12 sickles, and 4 plows. Every mission also had a *carreta*, which was a two-wheeled cart, pulled by oxen.

Original reports show that the Santa Clara mission was also given 4 hogs, 20 hens, and 3 roosters, along with cattle, sheep, goats, pigs, burros, horses, and mules. Mission Santa Clara de Asís seemed to have everything it needed, but it was still missing one major component— the participation of the local Indian population, the Ohlone.

◀ *A wooden cross marked the site of the mission.*

Work on the church began soon after the founding. ▶

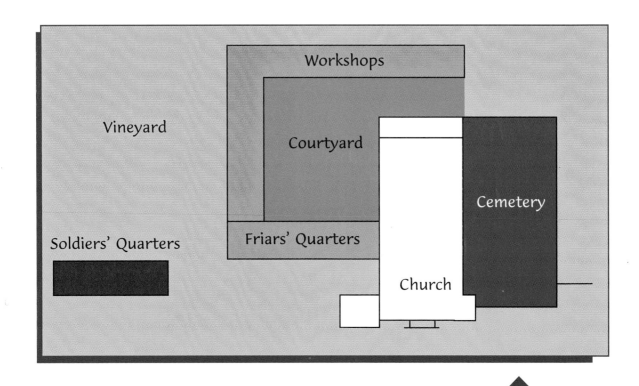

The layout of the mission buildings in the 1830s.

Building Santa Clara

The church was one of the first buildings to be constructed at each mission. The other buildings were built in the shape of a quadrangle around the church, forming a courtyard in the middle.

The Santa Clara mission had living quarters for the Catholic missionaries, a dining room, workrooms for weaving cloth, tanning hide and other trade, dormitory-type rooms for unmarried boys, and a separate place for unmarried girls, called a *monjerío*.

The missionaries needed the help of the Ohlone Indians for the actual building of the structures. They enticed them to work by offering food, glass beads, blankets, and other trade goods. The more the Ohlone Indians helped, the more gifts they received.

Under the Catholic friars' supervision, the Indians built the first church and living quarters of wood and thatch.

Converting the Ohlone

With shelter and protection provided, not to mention plenty of food offered by the missionaries, the mission was ready to take in the local Indians. As the Ohlone became comfortable at the mission site, the friars would encourage them to be baptized into the Christian faith. The missionaries also emphasized the beautiful Catholic ceremonies and music, which were similar to what the Indians had enjoyed with their own religion. This also helped encourage the Ohlone to adopt Christianity. Once the Ohlone were baptized and became neophytes, they were not supposed to practice their old religion.

The neophytes were told that they must live at the mission. Occasionally they might be allowed to visit their old villages. Some neophytes did not like this rule, or any of the rules that were imposed on them.

At Mission Santa Clara de Asís, the friars had a difficult time persuading the Ohlone to join the mission. They were friendly to the Spanish, but kept their distance. Soon after the church was built, disease swept through a nearby village, killing many of the Ohlone children. The missionaries took this opportunity to reach the Ohlone people.

When the friars heard of the widespread sickness, they went to the Ohlone villages to help. Spanish soldiers brought the sick children to the mission to care for them, and many of their parents came, too. These families were some of the first Indians to become neophytes at Mission Santa Clara de Asís. Despite its slow start, the mission recorded the most baptisms of any California mission, with 8,536 baptisms between the years 1777 and 1832.

The Many Sites of Mission Santa Clara de Asís

The original church of Mission Santa Clara de Asís was founded on the banks of the Guadalupe River. This was the first of five different sites for this mission. Within two years of the founding, the first church was flooded, and the missionaries were forced to move. They quickly constructed a temporary church while the mission compound, made of adobe, was being built.

Fray Serra was present for the laying of the cornerstone of the third church in 1781. The church took three years to complete, and when it was finished, Mission Santa Clara de Asís was known as one of the most beautiful missions in all of California. The third church of Mission Santa Clara de Asís contains the first painted decorations that are mentioned in any records, though no details were given as to its design. Its front had many fine details and intricate designs.

Unfortunately, after earthquakes in 1812 and 1818 destroyed the church, the missionaries were forced to move the church a fourth time. Again, this was a temporary site until the fifth church and connecting structures were completed in 1825.

The fifth church was ornately decorated, with its ceiling painted by the Mexican artist, Agustín Dávila. At many missions, the neophytes painted scenes and designs on the walls, but Dávila was brought to Santa Clara specifically to design the ceiling of the Santa Clara mission church. It features a circle of clouds with young angels peering down into the sanctuary. Other angels playing instruments dance among the clouds. The Trinity, which includes God the Father, God the Son, and God the Holy Spirit, are painted as three men sitting together. Dávila had neophytes paint these scenes under his guidance.

▲
This is the altar and original ceiling of the church at Mission Santa Clara de Asís.

The fifth church remained in good condition until 1926, when an early morning fire swept through its walls, burning it to the ground. The sixth and final church was built in the same spot, but this time the church was made of concrete to protect it from burning again. The beautifully painted ceiling was also destroyed in the fire, but a copy was made in the new church following the original design.

Only 4 of the 21 California missions were named after women. They are Santa Inés Virgen y Mártir, La Purísima Concepción de Maria Santísima, Santa Bárbara Virgen y Mártir, and Santa Clara de Asís. Mission Santa Clara de Asís is named for Saint Clare of Assisi, a nun from the 1200s, who worked closely with Saint Francis.

This is the picture that Agustín Dávila painted on the church ceiling. The group of three men represents the Trinity.

33

Daily Life

Life at the Santa Clara mission, as well as the other missions, varied little from day to day. Everyone's schedule was set by the ringing of the bells. Each mission had at least two bells. It is thought that one bell rang for work, mealtimes, and rest, while the other bell rang when it was time to pray or have devotions, which are short readings from the Bible.

The Ohlone Indians had never lived such a structured lifestyle. They were used to working when they needed to work and sleeping when they needed to rest. The missions changed that.

At sunrise, everyone went to the mission church to pray and sing. An hour later, the bell rang for breakfast. The rest of the day usually went like this:

7 A.M.	Bells rang to send the Indians to work.
12 noon to 2 P.M.	Indians ate their meal and had a *siesta* (a nap).
2 P.M.	Missionaries, neophytes, and soldiers returned to work.
5 P.M.	The missionaries led prayers and devotions.
6 P.M.	Supper was held for all, followed by free time.
8 P.M.	Bedtime for women.
9 P.M.	Bedtime for men.

Neophytes labored at many tasks, such as weaving, farming, tanning leather, and making tools in order to keep the mission running.

As with the other missions, gardening and farming were critical to the mission's survival. Mission Santa Clara de Asís boasted healthy, ripe crops of peaches, apricots, apples, pears, figs, and grapes. Even though the grapevines did not grow as well as the other crops, the wine produced from the grapes was considered good.

The bells rang to call the neophytes to work, prayer, and meals. ▶

Sometimes an expert in a particular field was brought in to help teach the neophytes a trade. In 1792, Miguel Sangrado, a tanner and shoemaker, came to Santa Clara, where he helped guide neophytes in the tanning of 2,000 hides that year. To tan hides, the workers first had to scrape every bit of meat off of them. Then the workers would hang the hides up on posts or stretch them and lay them out on the ground to dry. Once dry, they were sold to traders.

▲
Animal hides were hung and stretched like this one.

36

Neophyte women wove baskets as they had done when they lived in their villages. They also learned to weave blankets from wool. They made white woolen blankets with yellow stripes. While most dyes used at the missions were imported, the yellow color supposedly came from native wildflowers.

An Ohlone basket.

As the years passed and the growth of the mission's population slowed, many neophytes were given the task of recruiting other California Indians into the mission system. Some Santa Clara neophytes headed to the nearby *pueblo* of San José to find new converts. Others returned to their old Ohlone villages and to other tribes miles away to bring back new Indians to convert. Often, these new recruitments were brought to the mission against their will.

Many neophytes tired quickly of the mission and longed for their old way of life. Some would even try to leave the mission and escape to their own villages. Soldiers were sent to bring back these Indians. The neophytes were then beaten, jailed, or locked in shackles.

The neophytes who worked hard to please the missionaries were free from harm. The younger California Indians who had been raised within the mission system knew of no other life outside the white-walled church and its quadrangle. They didn't know about the days of fishing in the ocean or spending afternoons picking acorns or berries. The young did, however, hear grumbles from the older neophytes about

Cattle raising was the largest moneymaker for the missions. Mission Santa Clara de Asís was one of the most productive in this area, ranking 4th in livestock out of the 21 missions. Every mission had its own individual brand used to mark its cattle. This is the brand for Santa Clara's cattle.

their dissatisfcation with mission life. As the negative talk grew, so did the discontent among young and old alike. As the years passed, many Ohlone neophytes became more and more unhappy with their situation.

The Daily Life of the Missionaries

It was the friars' responsibility to educate the neophytes in the Catholic religion and the Spanish language. They led the young children in studies each morning and afternoon while the adults worked.

While the friars never gained financially from the Indians' work, they had to make sure the neophytes worked at a trade in order to keep the mission running smoothly. If the mission did not bring in enough money to support itself, it would be in danger of closing. The missionaries sometimes beat the neophytes who did not do their jobs, or when possible, had the soldiers dole out punishment. Understandably, this did not encourage good will between the neophytes and missionaries.

Troubles at Mission Santa Clara de Asís

Natural disasters in the area, including floods, earthquakes, and fires, caused Mission Santa Clara de Asís to be built six times in five different locations. However, it was trouble between the California Indians and the missionaries, as well as with nearby settlers, that caused the most severe problems at Mission Santa Clara de Asís.

The Pueblo of San José

In 1777, the year that Mission Santa Clara de Asís was founded, the *pueblo* of San José was also started by the Spanish. The *pueblo* was formed to be a farming community and to strengthen the Spanish presence on the coast. Those who lived there were often poor. From the very beginning, the people of the *pueblo* of San José and the residents of Mission Santa Clara de Asís did not get along. They argued primarily over land and water rights for their crops and livestock. Sometimes the livestock of the two groups mixed, which led to more disagreements. Eventually, they set up boundaries to separate the pastures where the animals roamed.

One of the missionaries who served at Mission Santa Clara de Asís, Fray Magín de Catalá, tried to draw the *pueblo* of San José and the Santa Clara mission together by building a four-mile road from the *pueblo* to the mission's church doors. Indians planted willow trees all along the road to provide shade and protect people from wild cattle. It took 200 workers to finish building the road.

When it was complete, the road was called the Alameda. While the road did not bring very many San José residents to Santa Clara,

The mission church had to be rebuilt many times because of flooding and earthquakes. ▶

except to attend church or bury their dead, it was a beautiful road that was used for decades. It has since been expanded and most of the trees have been replaced. Most of the occupants at the *pueblo* of San José never became friendly with those at the Santa Clara mission. It was a quiet, small town until the Gold Rush in 1848. San José then became the first state capital of California in 1849. It remained the capital until 1851. It has continued to grow, and today it is home to San José State University, the first state college in California, which was established in 1857.

Disease

The biggest problem at Mission Santa Clara de Asís, and at every other California mission, was the threat of disease for the Indians. When the Spanish came from Europe, they brought illnesses including measles, smallpox, pneumonia, and mumps. The Indians had never been exposed to these diseases. When they came in contact with them, thousands of Indians died. In fact, deaths due to these diseases resulted in the loss of hundreds of thousands of Indian lives. It is estimated that the California Indian population declined from 300,000 down to approximately 30,000 by 1850. Nevertheless, the descendants of the Ohlone and other California Indians still live in the state today.

According to official counts during the mission period, only 4 percent of neophytes who were lost to the missions were lost due to fugitism, or escape. The other 96 percent were lost due to death, almost all from disease.

◀ *Many neophytes were buried in the mission's graveyard.*

The Secularization of the Missions

Up until the 1820s, Spain owned all the missions and the land surrounding them. In 1821, Spain lost control of Alta California. New Spain revolted against its parent country and fought in a civil war for many years. After 11 years of fighting, New Spain became its own country. It was renamed Mexico. The Mexicans now owned Alta California.

Members of the Mexican government wanted the rich mission lands for themselves. They planned to send more people north to settle the area and make their country stronger. Government officials planned to secularize the missions, taking some land for these new immigrants to live on, and turning over other areas of land to its original inhabitants, the Indians. This would mean taking the missions away from the Franciscan friars and replacing them with parish priests, who would perform church services, but would not be in charge of the mission lands or neophytes.

The Spanish missionaries, who would lose all they had worked for over the past several decades, were strongly against secularization. They believed the neophytes were not ready to operate the mission lands on their own. The friars had changed the life of the Ohlone Indians, a self-sufficient culture that had lived undisturbed for centuries, into a group that had become dependent on the mission system for its livelihood.

While Mexico's original intention of secularization was to turn much of the missions' land over to the Indians, this did not happen. In April 1834, Mexican governor José Figueroa began secularizing the missions. Governor Figueroa did not plan to turn the valuable land over

◀ *The Mexican revolution.*

over to the California Indians. He expected the Indians to continue working in the mission fields, but they would not own them. Instead the land would belong to the government. The Indians' work was needed to make goods to sell in order to pay the salaries of the administrators under the governor.

Mission Santa Clara de Asís was secularized in 1837, and its buildings were left to fall apart. The Indians left the mission, leaving no one to take care of the structures, the crops, or the animals.

The Ohlone Indians who had lived at Mission Santa Clara de Asís were lost without the mission system. Those who tried to return to their villages found problems they'd never experienced. They couldn't hunt game because the livestock from the mission had driven them away. The Ohlone couldn't gather grass seed or acorns because the sheep and cattle had eaten the grass, and the oak trees, where acorns once abundantly grew, had been cut for fuel and to make furniture and other materials. The Ohlone did survive these changes and are an important part of the modern cultures that comprise the Bay area of Santa Clara today.

In 1850, during the presidency of Millard Fillmore, California became the 31st state in the United States. In 1851, a bishop from Monterey invited the Jesuit priest John Nobili to fix the mission's buildings and create the first institution of higher education in California. This gave the eighth mission a whole new purpose in the development of northern California.

President Fillmore was in office when California became a state. ▶

46

The Jesuits repaired the mission's buildings, and in March 1851, the doors of Santa Clara College were open. In 1912, the college was renamed Santa Clara University. Today, this college is still an institution for higher education, and Mission Santa Clara de Asís sits in its center. It is the only mission of all 21 missions to be a part of a college campus in the United States.

47

Mission Santa Clara de Asís Today

If you walk around the campus of Santa Clara University today, you can see the adobe lodge and adobe wall, the only parts of the original buildings that survived the 1926 fire. They were restored in 1981. Not only are they the oldest buildings on campus, they are the oldest buildings on any college campus in the west.

The front of the mission church features the original wooden cross of 1777 that was planted at its founding. It is now covered in redwood to protect it. Services are still held in the church sanctuary.

Around the campus, visitors can find grinding stones, 170-year-old olive trees, and hitching posts, which take them back to the days of a thriving, fruitful mission.

▲

The adobe lodge.

▲

The original adobe walls.

◀ *People like to visit Mission Santa Clara de Asís to learn more about California's early history.*

49

The original wooden cross from the mission's founding in 1777.

Father John Nobili, the first president of Santa Clara College, addressed one of the first goals of the college: "To cultivate the heart, to form and cherish good habits, to prevent and eradicate evil ones."

These words echo the beliefs of the Ohlone people who danced, played, worked, and ultimately died, on the same grounds that the university and Mission Santa Clara de Asís still rest on today.

While the mission system was meant to educate the California Indians, it had a much different outcome. The Indians lost their way of life, which had been successful for generations. The missions, though, did bring a new culture to the land, opening up California to the rest of the world. Today, the state of California is a leader in agricultural production, largely due to the work started by the Spanish and the Ohlone. California continues to be a state made up of many different religions and cultures, and the missions that dot its coastline are a reminder of its first treasured inhabitants.

▲

A bell along El Camino Real.

Make Your Own Mission
Santa Clara de Asís

To make your own model of Mission Santa Clara de Asís, you will need:

foamcore board
glue
miniature bell
brown, cream, red, and green paint

X-Acto knife (Ask for an adult's help.)
decorative flowers and leaves
paintbrush

Scotch tape
paper (white)
toothpick
Styrofoam crosses

Directions

Step 1: Cut a large foamcore board to measure 31″ by 44″ for your base. Paint it green. Let dry.

31″

44″

Step 2: For the front church wall, draw the dimensions as pictured below. Cut out with X-Acto knife. Cut out a window as shown.

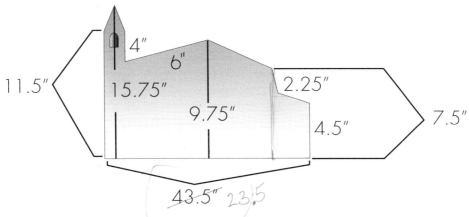

Step 3: Cut back church wall out of foamcore with dimensions pictured below.

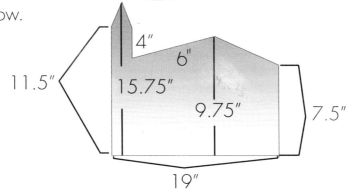

Step 4: Cut a piece of foamcore with dimensions of 7.5" by 18.5". This is the right side of the church.

Step 5: Cut another piece of foamcore to measure 11.5" by 18.5". This is the left side of church. Cut a piece of foamcore to measure 4" by 18.5". This is the right side of the bell tower.

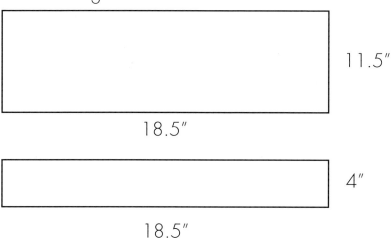

11.5"

18.5"

4"

18.5"

Step 6: Paint all walls with cream colored paint. Let dry. Tape and glue the inside edges of all church walls together. Set aside.

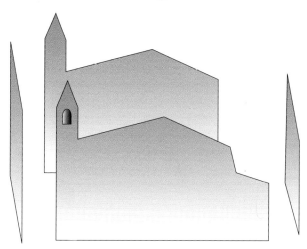

Step 7: Cut three pieces of foamcore to measure 3.3" by 18.5". These will be the outside walls. Paint with cream colored paint.

18.5"   3.3"

Step 8: Cut two courtyard walls (inside walls) out of foamcore to measure 4" by 18.5". Cut a courtyard wall (inside wall) to measure 4.5" by 13".

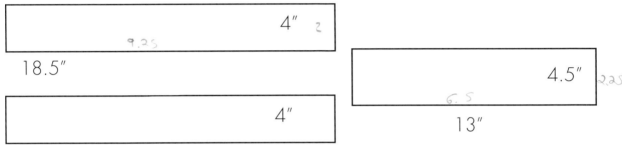

4" 2

9.25

18.5"

4"

18.5"

4.5" 2.25

6.5

13"

Step 9: Paint all the courtyard walls with cream colored paint. Set aside to dry. Put glue on the bottom of the church walls and glue to the green foamcore base.

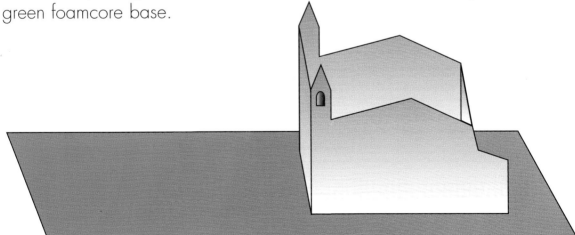

Step 10: Glue the courtyard walls in place on the foamcore board next to the church.

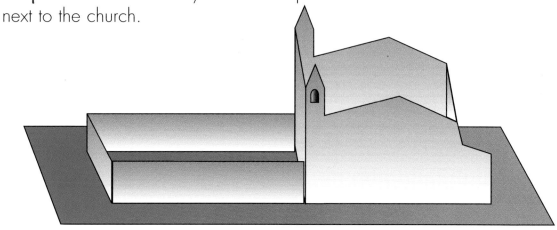

Step 11: To make the church roof, cut a piece of white paper to measure 14″ by 19.3″. Paint both sides red.

14″   14″

19.3″   19.3″

Step 12: Make the bell tower roof by cutting a piece of white paper to measure 10″ by 19.3″. For the extension roof, cut a piece of white paper to measure 4.5″ by 5″. Paint both sides red.

10″   4.5″

19.3″   5″

Step 13: For courtyard roofs, cut two pieces of paper measuring 3" by 18.5" and a piece measuring 3" by 13". Paint these red.

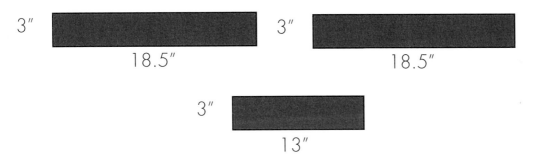

3"   18.5"   3"   18.5"

3"   13"

Step 14: Glue roofs to the tops of the courtyard buildings.

Step 15: Slide a toothpick through a miniature bell and insert into bell tower window. Decorate the mission with greenery and Styrofoam crosses.

*Use the above mission as a reference for building your mission.

Important Dates in Mission History

1492	Christopher Columbus reaches the West Indies
1542	Cabrillo's expedition to California
1602	Sebastián Vizcaíno sails to California
1713	Fray Junípero Serra is born
1769	Founding of San Diego de Alcalá
1770	Founding of San Carlos Borromeo del Río Carmelo
1771	Founding of San Antonio de Padua and San Gabriel Arcángel
1772	Founding of San Luis Obispo de Tolosa
1775–76	Founding of San Juan Capistrano
1776	Founding of San Francisco de Asís
1776	Declaration of Independence is signed
1777	**Founding of Santa Clara de Asís**
1782	Founding of San Buenaventura
1784	Fray Serra dies
1786	Founding of Santa Bárbara
1787	Founding of La Purísima Concepción
1791	Founding of Santa Cruz and Nuestra Señora de la Soledad
1797	Founding of San José, San Juan Bautista, San Miguel Arcángel, and San Fernando Rey de España
1798	Founding of San Luis Rey de Francia
1804	Founding of Santa Inés
1817	Founding of San Rafael Arcángel
1823	Founding of San Francisco de Solano
1849	Gold found in northern California
1850	California becomes the 31st state

Glossary

adobe (uh-DOH-bee) Sun-dried bricks made of straw, mud, and sometimes manure.

Alta California (AL-tuh ka-luh-FOR-nyuh) The area where the Spanish settled missions, today known as the state of California.

Baja California (BAH-ha ka-luh-FOR-nyuh) The Mexican peninsula directly south of the state of California.

baptism (BAP-tih-zum) A ceremony performed when someone is accepted into, or accepts, the Christian religion.

Christian (KRIS-chun) Someone who follows the Christian religion, or the teachings of Jesus Christ and the Bible.

convert (kun-VERT) To change religious beliefs.

crucifix (KROO-suh-fiks) A statue of Jesus Christ on the cross.

Franciscan (fran-SIS-kin) A communal Roman Catholic order of friars, or "brothers," who follow the teachings and examples of Saint Francis of Assisi, who did much work as a missionary.

friar (FRY-ur) A brother in a communal religious order. Some friars are also priests.

Jesuit (JEH-zoo-it) A member of the Roman Catholic Society of Jesus devoted to missionary and educational work.

missionary (MIH-shuh-nayr-ee) A person who teaches his or her religion to people who have different beliefs.

neophyte (NEE-oh-fyt) The name for American Indians once they were baptized into the Christian faith.

New Spain (NOO SPAYN) The area where the Spanish colonists had their capital in North America and that would later become Mexico.

quadrangle (KWAH-drayn-gul) The mission buildings that form a square around a central courtyard.

secularization (sehk-yoo-luh-rih-ZAY-shun) When the operation of the mission lands was taken from the church and given to the government.

tule (TOO-lee) Reeds used by American Indians to help build their homes.

viceroy (VYS-roy) The governor who rules and acts as the representative of the king.

Pronunciation Guide

carreta (kah-RAY-tah)

informé (IN-for-maay)

monjerío (mohn-HAYR-ee-oh)

pueblo (PWAY-bloh)

siesta (see-EHS-tuh)

temescal (TEH-mes-cal)

ALAMEDA FREE LIBRARY

Resources

To learn more about the California missions, check out these books, Web sites and museums:

Books

Kuska, George and Barbara Linse. *Live Again Our Mission Past.* Larkspur, CA: Art's Publications, 1998.

Chapman, Cristina Alviso. *California Historical Society Quarterly.* 38(2): 101-111, 1959.

Levy, Richard. *Handbook of North American Indians, Vol. 8* California. Washington, D.C.: Smithsonian Institution, 1978.

Web Sites

http://library.monterey.edu/mcfl/mission.html
http://www.ca-missions.org/links.html
http://www.escusd.k12.ca.us/missiontrail.html
http://anza.uoregon.edu

Museums

De Saisset Museum
Santa Clara, California
(408) 554-4528

Index